LISA DWYER

GOD IS TALKING

Road Signs: God is Talking

Copyright © 2021 by Lisa Dwyer. All rights reserved.

Published By:
MD Press
roadsigns2020@gmail.com

All rights reserved: This book is protected by the copyright laws of the United States of America. No part of this book may be reproduced in any form or by any means, electronic or mechanical, including photocopying, recording, informational storage or retrieval systems, without written permission by the author, except where permitted by law, for the purpose of review, or where otherwise noted.

Unless otherwise noted, Scriptures are taken from the NEW KING JAMES VERSION®. Copyright© 1982 by Thomas Nelson, Inc. Used by permission. All rights reserved.

Scriptures marked NIV are taken from THE HOLY BIBLE, NEW INTERNATIONAL VERSION ®. Copyright© 1973, 1978, 1984, 2011 by Biblica, Inc.™. Used by permission of Zondervan.

Book Creation and Design
DHBonner Virtual Solutions, LLC
www.dhbonner.net

ISBN for Paperback: 978-0-578-86541-6

Printed in the United States of America

For Mom...
Thank you for always believing in me.

Acknowledgments

Pastor Maggie McKinley, for many years I sat in church taking notes while you preached. I used long, white envelopes, writing the date and message title at the top, and the notes below. When you dropped in a personal golden nugget, I would write "PM" and circle it, so I knew it was your quote. I still have a collection of them in my dresser drawer that I reference from time to time, and it transports me. Those sermons imprinted my heart, and the lessons are ever with me. You will always be a special person in my life. Thank you for teaching me to always look to the Word of God. I'm grateful to know you as a Pastor, friend, and mentor in the faith for all these years.

> "Don't worry about anything; instead, pray about everything. Tell God what you need, and thank him for all He has done."
> -Philippians 4:6 NLT

Table of Contents

Acknowledgments v
What's Your Story? ix
Prove It! 1
Begging Dogs 5
Bright Lights 9
Buildings 13
Cars 17
Cracked Ice 19
Deafening Silence 23
Flavor Transfer 27
Frosty Morning 33
Humpty Dumpty 35
Internet Connection 39
What's Your Logo? 43
Makeshift or Connection? 47
Navigation 51
Picture This 55
Playground 59

Rainbow	61
Raindrops	63
Road Trip	67
Road Signs	73
Roly-Polies	77
Square Peg, Round Hole	81
Shipping and Receiving	85
Signs of Life	89
Sunflowers	93
Sunlight	97
The One Person	101
Traffic Jam	107
Water Heater	111
Water Towers	115
Weeds and Seeds	119
Still On The Road...	121

What's Your Story?

Your life, the memories you make, and the wake your path leaves in life are your legacy; what an exceptionally powerful thing that can be for others. You can spend years together with someone, and when your time with that person ends, perhaps only a handful of memories remain indelible—so it was with my mother. The thing I value most about my time with her is the way she influenced my faith in God. She always defaulted to her faith in God and so impressed me that I do the same.

I'll never forget listening to her as I laid across the foot of her bed while she sat in the chair across from me, watching her tell the "apple" story for the first time. She told it like it was yesterday, and her face conveyed that because of it, she would never be the same. It was her story about what happened when at six years old, on a walk to town with her grandmother, she encountered God.

Mom's words painted the picture . . . we had a truck, but dad took it to work every day. Granny needed things from the store, so we headed out, walking to town. It was very hot, and I was thirsty; I remember being parched. Granny told me we'd be in town soon, so we just kept walking by the small ditch on the side of the road.

I thought about how good an apple would taste to quench my thirst, and I couldn't get my mind off of it. We were poor, so fresh fruit wasn't something we normally had at home. I wanted an apple so bad; I told my granny.

Next, I announced "If He wanted, God could give me a whole ditch full of apples." At this point, Mom's lips pursed so she could finish the story without crying. "About another block up the road, you'll never guess what happened. The ditch beside the road was FULL of apples — and a few potatoes mixed in too! God did that for me — to show a little girl how much He loved her." As she spoke, the depth in her eyes showed the love felt that day by a six-year-old girl. I asked her what happened. She finished the story, "I ate apples until I was full, and carried as many as I could. I was just sure by the time dad got home that night to take the truck and load up that they'd be gone, but they weren't! We went back, filled the truck, and I had all the apples I wanted!"

What a powerful story of her encounter with the Lord right there on the roadside; it was the beginning of her life-long walk with God and her legacy.

When Mom talked about God, it permeated; it was loving and personal to her. If you were the one listening, it was transferable. Through her, I learned that God is always the same. I learned that He is no respecter of persons. She told me that if He did it then, He could do it now. The Bible is full of personal experiences like Mom's. They are just in a different time, at a different place and with different people. But if Mom is right and the Bible is right, time and place don't matter to God. He did amazing things over and over for people.

One that stands out in my mind was the day when Joshua and his army were in a battle, and Joshua asked God to make the sun and moon stand still so they could finish. God answered his prayer (Joshua 10:12-14). How incredible that God caused the sun and moon to stand still to honor a prayer! Equally fantastic is the account of Shadrach, Meshach, and Abednego, who were put into a fiery furnace but did not die from it. Jesus' presence was seen in the fire, and the men emerged alive, and their clothes didn't even smell like smoke (Daniel 3:16-30)!

Those stories and others were recorded to increase our faith, so we know that God is able. Life-altering moments come, and we don't even know they are about to happen, but in a blink of an eye, God saves us or indelibly touches us. Our stories, much like the six-year-old girl named Janice, become a witness and testimony to God's existence.

The entire Bible is a movement of God interacting with man and the stories left to tell. He is still interacting with us. Hebrews 13:8 says that God is the same yesterday, today, and forever. That means He is still speaking. A God who spoke through a burning bush, through donkeys, used Angels as messengers, and spoke to men through a voice from Heaven isn't suddenly powerless to do the same today.

I've heard many people ask how they can tell when God is speaking to them. There isn't one answer, but there are ways to know when you hear Him. When you take time to learn about God, you will recognize Him. If you are not in a relationship with God, His characteristics are recognizable through the fruits of the spirit found in the Bible (Galatians 5:22-23). Even people who don't want a relationship with God recognize His earmarks.

It is the love of a perfect parent and the good voice, encouraging voice, that whispers goodness into your heart. It is the gift of little treasures stored inside of you. It is also the correcting voice telling you the things you should or should not do for your sake. When you know what you're about to do is wrong, and you reason with the inner voice to feel better about giving in to a bad choice, you aren't arguing with yourself! Sometimes, it is a nudging — a time when everything within tries to direct you to do something that just doesn't make any sense at all. God's way doesn't always sound reasonable to us, yet it is in our best interest.

His voice is never destructive. Biggest tip of all? He is His Word. If you read the Bible, you learn about God, who He is, and what He represents. Then, when you hear something inside your heart that you think is Him, and it lines up with His Word, you realize . . . yup, that's God!

Every day, God shows me something and speaks to me about His profound love, along with His mercy and grace. I see it all around me in the road signs of my life. In the following pages, I have shared some of them. It is my reverent prayer that you be inspired to take a closer look, finding the signs God designates for you, and develop a closer relationship with Him. He's waiting for you to find Him. Your stories wait to be told.

God is most definitely speaking. Are you listening?

Prove It!
The drive begins...

While driving to Waco today, I was thankful for the gorgeous Texas sunrise. As I approached the nearby town of Belton, I saw a thick fog in the distance hovering over the land to my left. I realized, wow, that must be the lake! Although I knew it was somewhere in that general direction, I had never seen it from the road before and couldn't possibly see it at this distance. But the fog represented what must be the lake, and there it was presenting itself to me. It was a sign that it was there.

That was awesome to me! The multi-colored orange sunrise, the trees, and the fog were a living picture. Once again, something was reminding me of God. We don't see God, but He is there, and so many things in our lives give testimony to His existence.

It reminds me of times as a kid when someone would tell an unbelievable story, and our response was "prove it!" Proof positive is not always possible. Why is it that so many people either question or deny the existence of God because they can't see Him? There are hundreds of things we do every day, putting our trust in the unseen without giving it a second thought.

Obviously, there is a difference between the physical and spiritual, but follow these thoughts for a moment. Think about elevators. People use them without a second thought. They can't see the cable systems that hold the elevator, yet they believe that when they get in and push the buttons, it will take them to their floor. Another thing people place their trust in is their cars. They get into their vehicle, turn the key, and put it into drive, believing that it will move forward; they trust the components will make it happen. Computers, stoves, appliances, plumbing, and electricity... we trust these things to work without being able to see what really makes them function. People believe in their power.

How about something more subtle? How about someone who has the job of raising a flag each morning? They run the flag up, believing it will fly. Some days it flies higher than others, but nonetheless, it will lift with the wind. The wind isn't something that is seen; only the evidence and effects of the wind can be seen.

An extreme example is carbon dioxide. You can't see it, touch it, or smell it, but it is real and can be deadly.

Enter God. The existence of God can be neither proved nor denied. It is much like love. Love isn't tangible, yet people live and die for love each day. It is an emotion that drives people to do both wonderful and crazy things. Yet if you ask someone to prove their love for you, how can they do it? You can't "see" love, and you can't always make sense of love. People can only demonstrate their love for you; it is by their actions and what they do for you, nothing else. It is up to you and whether or not you choose to believe that person's love for you. Very simply, it is a matter of choice.

Much like the fog was a sign for the lake that day, I trust in things to work without seeing the components, are the signs in my life. They weave an unseen tapestry connecting my heart to God's. It is my choice to believe.

DOUBTING THOMAS?

Some people are just a Doubting Thomas. This is the expression used for people who refuse to believe something without seeing it firsthand. You know, the "I've got to see it to believe it" person?

But what if you can't see it? You can't actually see everything that exists. Some things are invisible to the naked eye. That's when it becomes about choice. Giving your life away into eternal uncertainty is a huge gamble that can never be reversed; you can't change that bet. Just what does it take to believe?

Think about it . . . it's not far-fetched. Most people leave a will for what happens to their personal belongings when they've gone — what arrangements were made ahead of time for what happens to their spirit? It is too late once they're gone.

In the beginning, it's about what God shows us. In the end, it's the choice we make and what we do with what He's shown us. Of all the choices we make in life, it is the one that counts more than any other. As for me, I choose to go to my Father's house!

Heavenly Father, thank You for the signs of life You put in my path. Thank You for opening the eyes of my understanding so that I can see the truth and accept it as You speak to me. Thank You for showing me the way through other people's stories, the power of Your Spirit, and through Jesus. Thank You that my life is hidden in You.

> "In My Father's house are many mansions; if it were not so, I would have told you. I go to prepare a place for you. And if I go and prepare a place for you, I will come again and receive you to Myself; that where I am, there you may be also. And where I go, you know, and the way you know." -John 14:2-4

> Jesus said to him, "I am the way, the truth, and the life. No one comes to the Father except through me." -John 14:6

Begging Dogs

It doesn't matter what time of day or where my dog is at when I go to get food; he hears me. I know that because he seems to magically appear in front of me while I am making the food or once I sit down with a plate. Today, I warmed up some leftover enchiladas as brunch, and just as I set my plate down on the side table, my dog showed up wagging his tail, looking at me with that cute beggar's look. I looked back down at him and told him he was sadly mistaken.

That didn't stop him. You see, he's learned that if he waits until the end, he will get to lick the plate or bowl. He tugs at my heart, and it is hard for me to resist. I've taught him a bad habit. So, because of that, when anyone has food, he begs. He thinks that everyone else will give to him just like I do, but the truth is they get mad at him for begging. He doesn't get the same favor from them. When the begging doesn't work, he just sits and waits. That is what he did today. I sat down in the living room chair to watch TV and eat the enchiladas, and he just waited. Today, he did not get a bite, and he didn't get to lick the plate. I'm sure he was disappointed.

Oddly enough, as much as he likes table food and will hold out for it, he even comes when it's his dog food being prepared. I get his little bowl down and set it on the counter. I think the "clink" of his bowl is the tell. He quickly appears right after it hits the counter, but he acts differently when I'm fixing his food as opposed to my own. He appears and stands wagging his tail, then sits down instead of following me anxiously. He knows the routine and that his bowl will go down onto the floor onto its spot just for him.

Today it reminded me of the biblical story about the Syrophoenician woman. She was a woman who was not from Israel, therefore, not considered one of God's chosen at the time. Still, she came to Christ wanting her daughter to be healed of a tormenting demon. The disciples asked Christ to send her away, but instead, Christ answered her with a parable of sorts, saying that it was not good to take the children's bread (the healing intended for God's own) and throw it to the dogs (the dog being someone besides God's own). But the Syrophoenician woman bowed down before Him and said that even the dogs feed on the crumbs that fall from the Master's table. With those words of faith towards Jesus, He gave the healing immediately.

Through reflecting on my life, I realized my pattern. You'd think I would have learned better by now. Still, I can be in need of something that I want from God but wait until I'm at my end before asking Him. It's much like the dog sitting there waiting for its Master to drop something, only I do not have to wait. I only have to ask my Master, not beg, and certainly not take crumbs! It happened a lot with my health. First, I went to the doctor, and then, when I didn't want to go through it anymore, I asked God.

That is so backward! God doesn't want us to wait until we are at our end — He wants to be there at the beginning. God always wants to be our first choice! Why would I come late to dinner and only get what is left over when I have been invited to sit at the Master's table?

ARE YOU A BEGGAR?

There have been times when I've begged God for something again and again . . . as if He didn't hear me. I believe that God's hearing is better than my little dog, who hears the clink. Maybe, just maybe, God is preparing something for me and getting ready to serve it to me.

I just have to be patient and know that it is coming when He is done.

There are specific things that belong just to me. However, I believe that out of God's grace, there are occasions when He shares even more than my own. It's when I receive what He had in store for me, instead of what my mind had conceived, and it's better than I imagined. Isn't it possible the same is true for you?

Dear God, thank You for not making me beg. Thank You that You have already given me provision in Your Word. You have given me the authority to use Your Word, to use it for payment on the things I have need of out of Your promises. Your warehouse of promises never comes up out of stock. I only have to use Your Word and believe it will deliver. I may have to wait for my promise, but remind me to wait patiently while keeping my eyes looking up towards my Master.

> "Then she came and worshiped Him, saying, "Lord, help me!" But He answered and said, "It is not good to take the children's bread and throw it to the little dogs." And she said, "Yes, Lord, yet even the little dogs eat the crumbs which fall from their masters' table." Then Jesus answered and said to her, "O woman, great is your faith! Let it be to you as you desire." And her daughter was healed from that very hour."
> -Matthew 15:25-28

Bright Lights

No matter where I go, I attract people who need to talk and people with a story. I've learned to embrace it. Recently, during a night event at a local outdoor pool and recreation park, one such person approached me.

I first noticed him after entering the park, when we were walking past each other, and our eyes met for a moment. Later, after everyone else in my party took off, I sat alone babysitting the picnic table where everyone had dropped their towels and drinks. The table was stationed near the lazy river, winding through the park. I watched as the people floated by, and that is when I saw him the second time. A few minutes passed, and he came back walking through the lazy river, talking as he approached.

He proceeded to exit the river by boosting himself over the side closest to our table. His obvious, momentary loss of balance and struggle to regain it, was typical of a person who'd had a few drinks. He took the few steps between the table and the river with his hand extended and said, "Hi, my name is Sam." I replied, "Hi Sam, I'm Lisa. Nice to meet you."

Sam had a pleasing countenance and a spark in his eyes. He began talking, even rambling, about who he brought with him to the park. One by one and detail by detail, I learned a bit of his story. He was here with his five grandchildren, and a great-grandchild was on the way. His eldest grandson was engaged to be married, and his fiancée was the one carrying the great-grandchild soon to be born. Specifically, to be born in October, and he said that was one thing he wanted to make sure he was around to see.

He dearly loved his eldest grandson, who was joining the Navy and going on active duty; in a couple of weeks, it would all be done. He gave a long pause. He said that his future granddaughter-in-law knew that he'd be there for her. Then he said, "I have a wife and two new daughters." Both of the girls were not yet teenagers. He had just married in April and was starting all over again since his own children were grown. Then he added that his wife was a little mad at him right now. He mentioned a worker of his had been injured recently and how it hurt him because his workers are like his own.

With each parenthesis of what he said, I saw a bit of his struggle to cope. However, throughout the conversation, he would mention, "I just keep praying." I would affirm, say something encouraging, nod, and let him keep talking. I said just enough that he knew I agreed with God and prayer. At last, he extended his hand once more, and I reciprocated, concluding with a good-bye handshake. When he took hold of my hand, he held it in a grip for a minute while looking me straight in the eye and said, "Thank you. I just needed someone to talk to . . . have a good night."

As Sam walked away, I could imagine what he was going through in life just from the pieces of what he shared. I realized that I had the opportunity to pray for him. I don't believe it was by chance that we met. I also believe that he was out of character when I met him and that he might wake up embarrassed by what he poured out of himself to a total stranger. He would have no idea that I'd be praying for him. Then, moreover, it occurred to me about the many foolish choices in my life.

I can distinctly recall a couple of times when I knew God but wasn't growing up in Him like I should, and two specific people who were in my life at that time. I know, that I know, that I know, they prayed for me. Now that I am at a different place in my life and spiritual walk, I can see it in retrospect — I know it in my heart. I am so grateful for their prayers and can only wonder how their prayers changed my life for good. I hadn't thought about it in a long time, but meeting Sam made me remember.

ARE YOU A LIGHT?

My dear friend and pastor, Maggie, used to say that people know where to go when they need to find the light. I think it's true. When people know someone to be a source of hope, strength, encouragement, or whatever Godly quality they may need, they head to the person that represents it. Take a completely dark room and let a minuscule bit of light find its way through, and it will be seen. Light always trumps darkness. They can't abide together.

Lord, You are a God of hope, of peace, and of love. It is my prayer that my life would be a reflection of all the goodness You have put in my life, and that would be my only focus. It is so easy to open my mouth and say anything but something positive. It is too easy to be negative, so I call upon the heavens. Lord, let Your light come forth when I open my mouth so that others see You and the darkness must flee.

> "Let your light so shine before men, that they may see your good works and glorify your Father in heaven."
> -Matthew 5:16

Buildings

Down the road from where I live, there is a house being built. Since I live close, I get to watch through every stage. Right now, it is just the beginning, and I have no idea which house plan it is or what it will look like when it's done. Every day, people are there working, but not the same people work on it all the time. The builder contracts the work out to different companies.

Through the weeks, while watching the building, I thought about the whole process. The contractor starts with his blueprints. At the chosen location, he brings in a company to level the land and build the pad. The electricians and plumbers come in to establish their lines. Then the cement is poured onto the pad, and this creates the foundation. Once the foundation is finished, framing takes place and roofing. Then more electrical and plumbing work is done. There are drywallers, painters, carpet layers, tile layers, masonry, clean-up crew, and even nurserymen to plant a yard. Finally, there is a finished house.

All of these different companies worked on the house through the weeks, each doing their part as directed. The builder always knew what the finished house would look like; he never doubted. From past experience, he placed faith in the contractors to do their job. But the different workers on the house may have only known their specific part, not knowing what the overall picture would be.

I realized that God has "built" me throughout the years, and He continues to build me. Even I don't know His final plans for me. But true to the contractor who has the blueprint which tells every person working on the building exactly what to do and where to place every last thing, is our God. It is in the Master's hands.

WHO'S YOUR BUILDER?

Everything physical has a spiritual counter. Your parents gave you physical life; you have a spirit, too. Who gives your spirit life? Do you ever feel like phases of your life are under construction, and you could just get it done? Don't worry; God has your plans.

Lord Jesus, I pray today, thanking You for being my spiritual builder. Just like a house can't be built without a foundation and framework, I can't be built spiritually without You. I know, Lord, I have to be built from the inside out and that without a healthy spirit, I am nothing. Build me from the inside, Lord. Let Your Word be my framework and foundation, and let Your light and peace be the finishing touches on my outside, so no one will doubt You are my builder.

"For we are God's fellow workers; you are God's field, you are God's building. According to the grace of God which was given to me, as a wise master builder I have laid the foundation, and another builds on it. But let each one take heed how he builds on it. For no other foundation can anyone lay than that which is laid, which is Jesus Christ." -1 Corinthians 3:9-11

Cars

On the way to work today, I was looking at the cars around me and watching how their wheels rolled along the pavement. I thought about cars and how we put so much faith in them to take us where we are going. There we sit in this machine, rolling down the road. I looked at the car beside me on the highway and had a funny thought of all the car parts vanishing, just to see the driver sitting there suspended in air, moving down the road, and I laughed at the image it conjured — like Wonder Woman's plane!

Almost as quickly, the movie about Indiana Jones searching for the holy grail came to mind. In the movie, he is in a cavern tunnel and comes to the place where the cave ends, and there is nothing but a huge chasm. He is standing at the exit, and the next entry he needs is across this chasm, but there is no way across. When he realizes that a leap of faith is what could get him across, he took a breath, closed his eyes and lifted his foot into nothing but air, and stepped out.

Instead of falling into the abyss below, his foot landed on what was unseen solid ground. He was able to walk across because of faith in the unseen. I smiled at the thoughts.

Truthfully, anything can happen; our faith in cars is flawed. With that thought in mind, I realized that, although the wheels are what physically holds my car up, my faith in the Lord is what I rest in as I travel along. I thought about the spiritual parallel from the Lord to my car.

TRANSPORTATION?

What or who carries you each day? Is it your feet, a car, or your bicycle? The truth is that even though we are carried in the physical, we can't forget that there is a spiritual side that needs carrying, too.

Dear Lord, today, help me to open the Bible and get into Your Word just like I would get into my car. Let me put on Your armor to encase me. Let me start up my day with prayer as the engine. As I go through my day, be my driver, Lord. If it rains on me, be my wipers. If I encounter darkness, let Your light be my headlight, piercing the dark. Set my speed, Lord. Give me the wisdom to brake when necessary. When I should turn left or right, give me the signal. Please, Lord, help me to go forward and even reverse if needed. Lord, if You are my driver, I do not need a compass or a map, for You will always bring me to my destination.

> "Faith is the substance of things hoped for, evidence of things not seen. For by it the elders obtained a good testimony. By faith we understand that the worlds were framed by the Word of God, so that the things which are seen were not made of things which are visible." -Hebrews 11:1-3

Cracked Ice

Yesterday morning, I went to take my sister to work, because it was an icy day, and she prefers not to drive in such weather. Outside in the driveway, my van windows were covered in a thin layer of ice. I got into the van, started the engine to warm it up, and my sister came out to scrape the windows. She walked over to my side of the van and began scraping ice away from the driver's window from the bottom up.

As I sat there in the icy van, every breath producing vapor, I watched her outside the window. I wondered how it would feel if I was actually trapped inside and saw someone breaking me free, chipping a little at a time? What an incredible feeling it would be to know help was coming! As I watched her hit upon the thin layer of ice, it cracked two or three inches, and the next couple of scrapes took it all away. Little by little, as the ice got chipped away, I could see part of the outside. Again, I thought about being trapped. My stomach quivered, and my heart sank as I delved into the thought of being stranded somewhere. I could only imagine how much hope it would bring to see help coming through the frozen pane. The more my sister chipped, the faster it seemed to go, and soon the ice was all gone. She put her face near the glass and smiled at me through the window — a complete rescue! My imaginary plight made me think about how a trapped person would feel to be free.

It is like so many of us in real life; only we don't realize it. We have put a coldness in us over hurts and situations that has frozen part of our hearts. Bitterness, envy, hatred, strife — whether we are aware of it or not, it is ice upon our hearts. We can't see through our lives clearly with the covering. Our love is trapped inside, waiting to be free. It is only when the ice is taken away that we can clearly see to navigate our lives.

Have you ever tried to drive with iced-over windows? It is all but impossible, but many of us try to drive our lives with iced-over hearts, and we stand a good chance of wrecking. God showed me this icy morning that the love of Jesus is the only thing that can scrape away the ice so we can be free.

GOT ICE?

Is there any ice in your life? If so, do you have a spiritual defroster?

If you don't, God is available for the asking. You know, ice can't melt itself. Get just a little bit of 'Son-light' on it, though, and the melt will begin.

Dear Lord, help me remember that when I can't see something clearly, I must have some ice on my heart. Help me to defrost my heart; come in and begin chipping away at my anger, hurts, and frustrations. Crack the ice, and then if only little by little, I can see the picture as the ice chips melt away. Lord, rescue me from the ice surrounding my heart, keeping my real love from reaching out to those around me. You are the only one with the tools to set me free.

> "The righteous cry out, and the Lord hears, and delivers them out of all their troubles." -Psalm 34:17

Deafening Silence

"*Deafening silence*" *is an* oxymoron — you can't go deaf "hearing" silence. Have you ever sat somewhere at home, at work, or in a car, with nothing going on around you, and you're left only with your thoughts? The silence can indeed be very "loud." So much so that we will distract ourselves to escape it. I think that we are so used to all the noise that silence scares us. Many people do not want to be alone with themselves.

In this generation, virtually everyone is plugged in - no pun intended; Facebook, Instagram, Twitter, TikTok, YouTube, gaming, cell phones, computers, televisions, and tablets. Most human beings, from babies to adults, are plugged in and on 24/7 in some kind of way.

The thing is, we don't hear ourselves, maybe can't even feel ourselves, and we certainly don't build a personal relationship between ourselves and God because that relationship is a personal, one-on-one thing.

Have you ever been in a conversation with someone who is distracted? How about a significant other? I know someone who refused to sit at the table and eat with her husband because he was on his phone, ignoring her. He did not value the time with her, so she got up and left the table. I worked for an organization that had monthly meetings, and when we got there, we had to place our phone (ringer off) in a clear, pocketed shoe holder in the front of the room, so everyone was focused on the meeting instead of arising distractions on their phone.

Personally, I left a large family gathering early because of phone distractions. After dinner, all my children and their spouses were sitting in the same room, everyone on their phones. There was no conversation between anybody. It was ridiculous. Everyone laughed at me when I made the comment "everyone is on their technology!"

Taking a call in the presence of others or texting during one-on-one time with another person, you essentially put the other person on hold, and create a barrier to them. That evening, I felt like I was alone in the room. The truth is we want to connect, and we want to be heard; God is no exception.

When we are constantly plugged into noise, we put God on hold. Sometimes all of the electronic mediums we choose are trojan horses that appear as an amazing gift to us, only to be filled with an army of things trying to destroy us from within.

For a relationship with God, we have to be quiet, read His Word, and be still in prayer without distraction so that we can hear His voice. It takes practice, but it comes.

HARD OF HEARING?

When we have been asking for something in prayer or wanting something from God, the absence of His direction, of His voice, feels deafening. I think it is His way of drawing us nearer to

Him. When we are desperate for an answer to a problem, we seek Him all the more. The Bible tells us that He is ever-present, so we know He is there. I believe that when we can't hear Him or feel Him, it's His way of drawing us in to seek Him all the more.

It's kind of like 'come a little closer and let Me whisper something in your ear.' You have to be close together and intent on hearing what is said. When we get that near to God, He can whisper into our hearts. Often, we are praying and seeking Him alone, when we first hear what He wants to say.

Lord, You are the source and supply of all life-giving things. The Bible tells us that. Today, help me choose the things that are important to You and important to my life. I know that if I put You first, all things will follow. Help me to unplug from all the distractions around me and focus on You. Help me learn Your voice and Your way, so I am able to hear when You call.

> "Be still, and know that I am God; I will be exalted among the nations, I will be exalted in the earth!" -Psalms 46:10

Flavor Transfer

Recently I hosted a kick back for a group of employees. It was the second anniversary of the business I manage, and I wanted to show my appreciation to every person and what they bring to the table. Outside near a greenway, we set up a small tent with food tables and chests of drinks. We put out yard games, a photo booth and played music by request. On the grass beneath tall pine trees, we put out blankets for people to sit, eat and talk.

As people arrived, they put their dessert contributions on a banquet table in the food tent. It was the completing element to our gathering. One young lady brought some delectable cookies. They were nicely prepared from scratch and bagged in pairs, both chocolate chip, and peanut butter cookies. At the end of the event, as we were cleaning and putting things away, I filled my truck that was parked nearby. When I discovered that there were a couple of bags of peanut butter cookies left, I took one and put them in the drink cup holder between my seats as a snack for the ride home.

I finished filling the truck cab, and knowing it was a mistake, I took my empty roaster pan and put it on the back floorboard without washing it. The pan had pulled pork stuck on it, and I thought I'd soak it when I got home.

When I was done with the outside clean up, I went inside to help my team finish their work, about two more hours, before heading home. I called to talk to my daughter on the way and was interrupted by a 1-800 number. I thought it strange to get a random call near midnight, so I didn't answer. Then my daughter on the other end of the line told me she was getting a call from my alarm company. Suddenly, I realized that was the call I'd ignored. She hung up with me and intercepted their call.

I was nearing home when all this happened and was passed by a speeding police car with lights on, which I found stopped at my house. A second police car pulled up, and the men asked me to unlock the door so they could enter my home. They went in guns raised, voices raised, "Police! Hands up! Police! Hands up!" They left no room, closet, or shower unchecked. Gratefully, it turned out to be a false alarm from a security system issue, but in all of the commotion, I only retrieved my purse from the truck that night. I left all the rest, including the roasting pan, until morning.

The next day, as I unpacked the truck, I saw the cookie bag I'd left in the cupholder. I had eaten one cookie on the drive home and left one for later. A prize for me for having this dreaded unloading task, I thought. So, I reached into the bag, broke off a piece, and plucked it out. As I closed my mouth over the cookie, I noticed something odd. The cookie was still sweet and peanut butter, but it had another flavor on it. Ever had a pulled-pork -flavor- peanut butter cookie? Well, that is what I had! I recognized the taste, and even though the cookies had never touched the roaster pan, somehow, through the small opening I left in the baggie, the smell of the pulled pork had flavored the cookie!

It is quite a phenomenon to me that just the aroma of a strong food can transfer flavor to other food around it. Nevertheless, we all know it happens. Almost immediately, I thought about the party and all the people, and a spiritual parallel came to mind: The true "flavor" of each of those employees and how they can permeate each other. Each one of them holds a special contribution that only they possess. Good, bad, or indifferent, they possess unique qualities.

That evening, as they visited with each other and contributed to each other, the outcomes could be many. The strong ones easily rub off on weaker ones. If the strong personality is one of hope, reason, inspiration, and edification, the outcome for the lot is good. But if the strong voice is one of despair, scoffing, intimidation, or belittling, the outcome could be bad. My parents used to quote a beloved pastor who said, "You have to teach children to be good; they know how to be bad all by themselves."

Reflecting on the night, I hoped all of the strong, positive voices were the flavor champions of the evening because I wanted the outcome for the lot to be good. Mixing flavors can be a risky business; you have to have the right recipe for good results.

WHAT'S YOUR FLAVOR?

Everyone has a circle of influence. Do you consider the impact you make on other people while you are talking?

Whether it's at home with family, at work, or somewhere else, people are listening to your words and learn from what you say. Your encounters with other people leave an impression. Have you ever heard the expression "It left a bad taste in my mouth" to describe a bad experience? Given a choice, those experiences are not ones you would repeat and are not easily forgotten.

You can't control anyone but yourself. You can choose your words carefully. You can choose not to listen to the scoffer and to raise your higher voice instead. You can choose God. Allow Him to be seen in you, invisibly mentoring others to do the same. Be salt and light.

Dear God, I acknowledge You as my Lord today, asking You to be my Leader. The Bible says to acknowledge the Lord in all our ways, and He will direct our path. Even more than that, Lord help me to control my words. Words can build up, and they can tear down, and we can never be certain of what we are doing unless our words are Your Words. Through You, help me to enrich lives and the spirits of those around me with words of encouragement and hope. The Bible says in Matthew 12:30 that we are either gathering or scattering; I choose to gather. Please remind me each and every day that my words can do both. The choice of influence is mine, and I am accountable to You.

"Do not be misled:
"Bad company corrupts good character."
-1 Corinthians 15:33 NIV

"Death and life are in the power of the tongue, and those who love it will eat its fruit." -Proverbs 18:21

"He who is not with Me is against Me, and he who does not gather with Me scatters abroad." -Matthew 12:30

Frosty Morning

It's a twenty-four-mile drive to the county seat where I was headed to answer a jury summon. It was chilly this early morning, but I didn't realize it was cold enough to freeze.

Then, about eight miles outside of the city limits, I saw frost along the roadside and a sign saying, "Watch for ice on bridge." I checked the temperature reading; sure enough, it was twenty-eight degrees. The open flat land here, unlike our city surrounded by hills, makes it subject to the worst of the weather, whatever the form.

I enjoyed the scenery of country homes and livestock roaming the land. Like any countryside, it was dotted with lavish homes and some near impoverished homes. I came upon a small spread of an old Airstream trailer, a painted mobile home, and other small outbuildings. There was an old car or two. It sat back off the road quite a way, and the entire area was covered by white frost, the sun gleaming on it except where a shadow or two were cast from the trees. Without the covering frost, the scene wouldn't have called for a second glance. However, with the white frost, the sunshine struck it in such a way that it was beautiful. Immediately the Lord brought to mind a spiritual truth. The scene is like us: In our own right, we are nothing for the Lord to look upon.

It is only the blood of Jesus that can cover us and wash our sins as white as snow. He only sees the beauty, not what lies beneath.

ARE YOU COVERED?

Who covers your mistakes? There are spiritual mistakes and bad choices that are way too big for humans to cover; there is no way we can. There is unacknowledged sin that separates us from God. Will you allow Christ to cover you and build a bridge into your life?

Dear Heavenly Father, thank You for the Blood of Jesus and for giving us a never-ending pardon from our sins. I am so grateful that He covers my sins and that covering is everlasting. It is not like the frost that will melt away and reveal the true things that lie beneath. Instead, with Jesus living in our hearts, the covering lasts forever, and You see us as beautiful as You would see Your only Son.

> "Come now, and let us reason together," says the Lord, "Though your sins are like scarlet, they shall be as white as snow; though they are red like crimson, they shall be as wool."
> -Isaiah 1:18

Humpty Dumpty

When I am driving, I often listen to podcasts. Today, I was listening to a well-known minister, and he was talking about a time when he was so broken that there wasn't anything left of him to break. He said that God told him that didn't matter because He was still able to put him back together. Almost immediately, my mind left the podcast and took me back to a day in time about five years ago regarding a particular incident. I was working in the Nutrition department at a local school district, and for some reason — I can't remember why — we were celebrating eggs. The director told us that if we brought in a decorated egg, there would be a contest for the most original, and the winner would get a gift card.

It was customary after closing our individual cafeterias to drive to the main office and deliver our paperwork. On one of those days, I needed to see our director about something, so after sorting and delivering the paperwork to its designated spots, I went to see her. I stood just inside the door of her small office, in front of the desk, as we talked. As our conversation concluded, she nodded towards her desktop for me to see an egg that was sitting there. It was the most gorgeous hand-carved, hand-painted ostrich egg I think I've ever seen. It was sitting atop a holder. As I gasped, the words "Oh, how beautiful" and lifted my hands to cover my mouth in amazement, my hand knocked the egg off onto the floor. I stood there watching the split-second accident in progress, then stared at the floor at what seemed like a hundred small pieces and wanted to cry.

In the shock of it, Humpty Dumpty came to mind, and it made me want to laugh at the same time I felt like crying. Embarrassed, I blinked back the tears and just kept apologizing. My boss, the wonderful lady that she was, said, "Oh, it's okay!" She mentioned it was cracked anyway, and she grabbed a box top off a new box of manila folders, and we began putting the egg pieces inside.

Scrambling for how all this would end, I told my boss that I would break the news to the owner of the egg. My boss wouldn't have it. She said, "No, I will tell her." She extended nothing but grace to me over what had happened. She then piped up and said that her daughter loved intricate work and she'd give it to her to fix. My mind couldn't imagine that all those fragments would ever resemble the original egg again, but she assured me that if anyone could do it, it would be her daughter. Knowing I didn't have a choice but to agree, I accepted with the stipulation that I would supply the glue and tools for the repair. In the next couple of days, I bought special glue and paintbrushes at the local craft store and took them to my boss. I walked out that day, not knowing what would happen, but I had done all I could.

When I was in her office the following week, it was the same scenario. She motioned with her eyes in a quiet smile towards her desk once more. There sat that ostrich egg, just like the first time I saw it; I could not even see the repair lines from where it was cracked. It was unbelievable what her daughter had done. I was truly amazed. To this day, I wouldn't believe it if I had not witnessed it with my own eyes. The flashback ended, and my mind returned to the podcast.

As I drove listening to the podcast and remembering the story, I realized that God is truly able to do that for us. We can be in one million pieces, and He can pull us all back together.

We can't see it for ourselves, but much like the egg, He knows what can be done. In the Bible, the spirit of the Lord showed Ezekiel a vision of dry bones (Ezekiel 37). In it, God resurrected a valley of dry bones, causing tissue and sinews to grow on them, and life breathed into them until there was a living army.

It is too hard for us to imagine, but with God, all things are possible. Even when something is our own fault, and we confess our mistakes to God over and over, asking forgiveness, all He does is extend us grace and answer our brokenness.

ANYONE BROKE?

Our God is a resurrection God. He specializes in bringing life to what is dead. He is able to resurrect our hope, our dream, our vision of our future with Him as the lead. He is a redeemer; it's what He does. God gives life to us. The Bible is clear that Jesus came to give us life, and the enemy comes to steal it.

If you feel like your life is in a Humpty Dumpty moment, let the one and only true King put you back together again.

God, I acknowledge You as my Lord and Savior. No one can help me like You, my Maker. You know me inside and out. So, I lay everything at Your feet today. What I have messed up, I ask You to fix. Give me wisdom, God, to go forward and build my life with You as my Leader. Redeem me from sin and past mistakes. Light my path, watch my mouth, give me instruction and the discipline to trust in Your plans for me. My hope is in You. Amen.

> "For You formed my inward parts; You covered me in my mother's womb. I will praise You, for I am fearfully and wonderfully made; Marvelous are Your works, and that my soul knows very well." -Psalm 139:13-14

> "The thief does not come except to steal, and to kill, and to destroy. I have come that they may have life, and that they may have it more abundantly." -John 10:10

Internet Connection

How many of you have been frustrated because your internet would not connect? Recently, I bought a laptop computer. It has built-in wireless internet capabilities, and I have wireless service, so I thought connecting would be a breeze. I was wrong about that. No matter what, I couldn't get it to work. My laptop detected wireless networks but wouldn't link up to them. It became very frustrating.

I spent over two hours on the phone in two different sessions, with both the manufacturer of the computer and my internet provider. At the end of the calls, there was no resolution to the problem. I took matters into my own hands, changing the service provider in order to get connected.

It was an arduous process. After it was all over, I could almost hear God say, "Why don't people go to those lengths to stay connected with me?" It stung down to my core; it is so true!

When it comes to matters of the heart – our physical heart, our own desires — we go to great lengths to get what we want. Whether it is internet service, a lover, friend, an education, or even a job, we bend over backward to keep these physical connections established. Yet when it comes to a spiritual connection with our Maker, the whole reason for which we're designed, we stop before we even start.

Excuses for this abound: I'm too tired; I'm too weak; too disappointed in man; too let down by churches; unwilling to answer God's call. God has heard all of this and more. He is there waiting — a free provider and divine spiritual connection, with more power than any other. The only problem with connectivity we'll ever have is that we won't link up or look for His signal.

Matters of this physical realm are for a limited time only, while the spiritual matters extend through this lifetime into ever after. I am not an experienced investor, but even I know that reward comes from long term investments.

WIRELESS POWER?

Have you ever felt powerless? How about disconnected? In the twenty-first century, that has a whole new meaning. People literally connect via powered devices. No matter where you go these days, outlets are everywhere so people can keep their devices charged and stay connected. But man needs to charge himself, too.

Mankind is the original design for wireless power. We are part of a network belonging to the biggest Power House in the universe. All we have to do is use our prayer to connect, and wait for power to flow into us from our Heavenly Father. For optimum operating results, a full charge is recommended.

Dear Lord, let me remember You each and every day. From the moment I wake up safely until I close my eyes the next time, let me think of You and all You provide. When my heart beats, and my lungs fill, and my eyes see, and I am breathing — a living and working being — let me remember my Designer. Let me remember, God, that I was designed to receive love; that I was designed to receive Your power from on high. Remind me, Lord, to keep plugged into You so that I always am fully charged by the power of Your might and help others remember to plug in as well.

> "Behold, I send the Promise of My Father upon you; but tarry in the city of Jerusalem until you are endued with power from on high." -Luke 24:49

What's Your Logo?

Signs are around us all the time. In public places or on the road, look around, and you see signs blaring with messages begging to be read. Driving to an appointment today, I noticed some unusual signs and started paying attention to the sheer number of billboards and signs; there were hundreds of them. Then I noticed that one thing most of the signs had in common was a company logo. Take your pick from food, retail, healthcare, or anything in between — it was there. The logo made the sign immediately recognizable, even from far away.

It's funny how a company creates an emblem, their mark, that will forever represent what it stands for. On the highway, there are exit signs for "food", "gas" and "lodging", with company logos telling what you will find at that exit. It is like a big announcement for motorists.

People wear their own symbols, too: T-shirts that announce their opinion, wedding bands, piercings, tattoos, religious symbols, or simply how they display their signature style. Sometimes it is something more that makes us recognize people. We recognize certain individuals by their personality and how they act. There are those we know who will be happy and upbeat no matter what their day is like.

Then there are other people who are a mixed bag, and we never know what to expect. Some are down and sarcastic no matter what. These things become that person's own sign and personal logo — the one thing that makes them easily recognizable to those around them no matter what.

As a Christian, there is something that is called *Logos*. Not logo, but Logos, which by definition means the divine Word of God. This is what I want to make me recognizable — the love of God forever within me. Because if it is truly written in my heart, I believe it is the one thing that makes me different, the thing that makes me shine, the thing that draws people to me when they need help, or prayer, when they wouldn't go to anyone else. It is not me, but God within me, and that is the logo I want people to see.

WHAT'S YOUR SIGN?

Ever seen someone with a "kick me" sign on their back? It was a prank I saw in school when I was growing up. It was funny most of the time. Like the "kick me" sign, most of us wear invisible signs that help determine how we are treated. What would yours say? I don't believe any of us can see ourselves as others; it's just not possible.

However, we can begin to make our own sign by the way we talk, the way we act, and simply being aware that the way we interact with those around us leaves marks.

Heavenly Father, I'm so grateful for Logos, the divine Word of God. It is my prayer that it will light me up from the inside out and be a beacon to those in need so I can share Your love and Your Word hidden in my heart. Let me be mindful each day as I leave my house to be looking out for the one You put in my path, waiting for a word of hope. Help me to be mindful that as long as You are in me, I never draw from a dry well, but You supply the needs of all. Gift me with words of truth, encouragement, and Agape love.

> "There was a man sent from God, whose name was John. This man came for a witness, to bear witness of the Light, that all through him might believe. He was not that Light, but was sent to bear witness of that Light. That was the true Light which gives light to every man coming into the world." -John 1:6-9

Makeshift or Connection?

Isn't it amazing how easy any job can be if you use the right tools? Have you ever used a butter knife or coin to drive in a flat head screw? I know I have. I can't tell you how many times I have used the heel of a shoe to drive a nail into a wall. Those things work, but not as intended. A shoe can't really remove a nail, nor can a coin as easily pull the screw back out once tightened; the connection is just not the same as with the right tool. But a screwdriver and hammer, the tools intended to do those jobs, does the job completely both ways.

The other day, I was at a locally owned auto repair shop of some folks I know, talking to the owner, when I looked over and saw a truck with the hood propped open with a rather big tree branch. I cracked up laughing. The owner looked over and cracked up with me and then gave the backstory. "You see, what happened was…" Too funny.

There are certain things in life that go together and have no purpose in and of themselves. Tools are one of those things. They are things that are designed for a specific purpose. Glue has no purpose by itself; it was created to join two objects together. Staples are the same. Scissors have no purpose of their own but are designed to cut things when needed.

There are other examples. Radio waves come from a transmitter yet need a receiver for the words to be heard. A power circuit has to have a receptor to prove there is power, whether it be a light bulb, an appliance, or an electric shock. The connection is the relationship between two objects. A nail, staples, glue, nor any of those things have a purpose by themselves. Those objects are designed to join things together. Even a boat has no purpose without water, and the list goes on.

Human beings have a purpose, and our design was specific. Our origin, our design, is to be the object of God's love. It is our purpose, and when we accept the love of Jesus Christ in our hearts, it makes the connection, joining us together with Him. God puts the love out there; we receive the love through Christ, and the connection happens. Receiving the love is man's choice. The love is there waiting to be received, and we are the receivers! So enters the power of choosing love and allowing it in our heart to be in a relationship with our Creator, who is infinitely bigger and wiser than ourselves.

MAKING DO OR CONNECTING?

There are some things we cannot create. When we need water, we must find a source. When we need food, we must find a source. The same goes for our spirit; we can't create what we need. When we need faith, hope, and grace in our lives, it has to come from something outside ourselves; it has to come from the intended source, our heavenly Father, and the Living Word of God.

Anything else is makeshift and will not work the same way. Remember, we are created for a purpose, and that purpose is to be a receiver of God's love. Man is created for God's love, and our purpose is fulfilled when we make the connection.

Dear Heavenly Father, teach me to walk in what I am called to do in this life. Help me to fulfill the purpose for which You called me to be: The object of Your infinite love. Remind me to take at least one waking moment each day, acknowledging You as my Savior, to set my path straight. I understand I am called not only to walk in Your love but to share Your love with others. Let me commit my work to You, so my thoughts are established.

> "We love Him, because He first loved us."
> -1 John 4:19

Navigation

One day, I had to travel to a neighboring city to pick something up from a specialty store. I was familiar with the city in general because I drive through it frequently, but I'd never seen that particular store. So, I called the store to get specific directions. A lady answered the phone, and I asked her if they had what I needed, and she told me yes. Then I asked her if she could explain to me how to get there.

When she started to tell me the directions, I recognized most of what she said. Then she named a street I didn't recall ever seeing; I even told her that. She assured me that they were there. I thanked her and got off the phone to head that way. As I drove, I thought it odd I had never noticed this specific street or store location.

It is about twelve miles between the two cities, so when I left my house, I drove a little slower than normal and paid particular attention to the signs. As a result, I found there were many things that I had never seen before; stores, side streets, and billboards, to name a few. I quickly realized how these must have been there all along, but I'd missed them.

Either I was going too fast or fixed on another destination to notice them before. Today, because I followed the specific directions I'd been given, I pulled up in front of the store I needed to find. I never knew it was there until I went looking for it.

That's how it is between God and us on our spiritual journeys. So many times, we are traveling along in our lives too fast to stop and call upon Him as our Navigator. Sometimes we are so fixed on a particular destination that we miss the lessons He has for us to learn. As a result, we travel through our lives without seeing the many things He placed in our paths.

God gives us signs and speaks to us, but unless we are looking for it, we will altogether miss it. We have to slow down, pay attention, and maybe even call upon Him for directions before we can get to the right destination. It isn't that God is missing; it is that we haven't been looking for Him.

DIRECTIONS, ANYONE?

There's an old adage about men that says they never stop to ask for directions, but thanks to technology, that has passed. We now have electronic navigation that directs us to specific geographical locations. But what about your spiritual location? What about the location of your heart, mind, and life? We were physically born into this world, but our spirit needs a navigator as well. We decide where we want to go, but God determines how we get there.

Dear Lord, help me begin my day. I ask You for directions before I start out; You are the only one who knows where the road will take me today. I ask that You open the eyes of my understanding to see the route You map for me and to recognize the signs You give me to follow. Help me so that I don't get fixed on my own road map or go so fast that I miss my turns and wind up at the wrong place. I put myself into Your hands, Lord, for You alone know my true destination.

"A man's heart plans his way: but the LORD directs his steps."
-Proverbs 16:9

Picture This

There was a cartoon circulating on social media that was spot on. It showed Noah's Ark sailing away from a shoreline. On the shore was a pair of animals staring at the Ark as it sailed off, and on the top of the Ark, all the animals were looking back at the pair still on the shore waving goodbye to them. The caption said, "It's all about your point of view." It made me laugh, but the point was clearly illustrated. A picture in a hotel room made me think about the same thing recently.

I met my family a couple of hours away from my home at a halfway point where they were planning to attend an MLB game. We all stayed together in a well-furnished hotel. Adjacent to the sink in the room's dressing area was an interesting picture. At first glance, I knew that it was a close-up shot of a leaf with some things, dots, on the edge. Initially, I thought the things were small bugs of some kind, but the dots that looked like bugs had some white on them. I decided they weren't bugs.

The second time I looked at it, I found myself wondering what the dots were, but shrugged and walked away. The third time, I decided to stand there and look at the picture and figure it out. Indeed, it was an extreme close-up of a leaf that showed the veins in the leaf, and at the edge of the leaf those little round things, several of them clinging to the edge. But what were the white dots on the round things; what were they? Then I saw it! They were droplets of water, and the white dots were the reflection of light on them.

Ah ha. Mystery solved.

Then I looked at the other half of the picture, which was really a green blur. It was all of the greenery; other leaves, a tree, a forest, that surrounded the one leaf. The background was blurry and out of focus because of the magnification of the one leaf. Immediately, God dropped the truth to me about perspective again.

When we are so focused on one thing, we forget about everything else. It's like focusing on the one leaf in the picture leaves the entire tree remaining to be seen. This is us. Many times, when we have problems, we allow them to become so magnified that we can't see everything as we should. We forget the context of our lives in God's hands. That leaf was attached to the tree, but you wouldn't have known it because it was out of focus.

We are rooted in God, sustained by Him. He is our life source, and all we are stems from Him. When we allow our focus to land solely on one thing, one issue in our life, the truth can become very distorted. When we focus only on one thing, we miss the other things that may be surrounding us in the whole picture. Those other things can be very important, just like that leaf that was still on the blurred-out tree, and that tree was sustaining its life. We must trust the Master behind the lens.

CAN YOU SEE CLEARLY?

Perspective is truly what it is all about, but sometimes it is hard to see any other perspective but our own. Our perspectives are shaped by many things — our emotions, life experience, wisdom, impatience, time, and so much more.

Our view is finite while God's is infinite. Wrap your mind around that before you choose to go it on your own and leave faith out of it. Human nature's propensity is putting intense focus on ourselves, but all we really are is part of a master plan. We are only one part of a multi-layered, multi-level plan. So, we must ask God and trust Him to show us our part — help us to do our part — and then the picture that bugged us, in the beginning, might just be a reflection of light in the end.

Heavenly Father, I know that Your perspective is always the spiritual one. In life, help me get the picture; help me to pause in all things and inquire of You, Lord. I ask You to remind me that I am only one part of a plan that I did not devise, so it is important that I ask first to know my part. Help me not to rush into any area or decisions without You, Lord, or before You light the way. Lord, don't let me be like Joshua, who did not inquire of the Lord, resulting in his making a covenant with the enemy. Let me always seek Your counsel first.

> "Then the men of Israel took some of their provisions; but they did not ask counsel of the Lord." -Joshua 9:14

Playground

The other day while running errands, I caught part of a Christian show on my car radio. A man was talking about how people question God's existence, citing that it isn't possible for God to hear their voice. He said people ask, "There are so many prayers, how can God possibly hear my one voice?" For me, it actually validated God's existence, yet I understood what the man was saying. It is a point of doubt for many people.

A few days later, I was at the park with my daughter. I sat nearby, drifting in my thoughts while she played on the equipment. I could hear the children laughing and shouting while they played. Suddenly, I heard a cry that gripped me. As I jumped up, I saw my daughter coming towards me with outstretched arms. I picked her up, checked to see if she was hurt, then kissed her tears away. I let her down, and she ran back to the playground again.

When I sat down and watched her climb the slide steps, it came to me immediately, and I knew the truth in my heart. Out of all of the children playing and shouting on the playground, when I heard my daughter's cry, I recognized it immediately.

I knew that it was her, began looking to find her and went to her rescue.

It also reminded me of a movie I watched. In the movie *Love Comes Softly*, a faith-doubting wife listens to her husband as he explained life's hurt. He said that if his daughter was walking beside him and she fell, it doesn't mean he caused her to fall or wanted her to fall, but it did mean he would be there to pick her up. That is how it is with God. He knows His children's' voices; any parent does. He hears us and is there for us when we call upon Him.

PLAYGROUND BULLIES?

Everyone needs protection from time to time. Is there some reason that you need to have someone watch over you? Not only our physical being but our spiritual condition needs a watchman.

Lord, I am so grateful that You watch over me. You hear my voice when I cry. You are faithful to hear me and come to my rescue. If I should stumble or fall, You are there to pick me up. Lord, I ask You to be my shepherd and keeper forevermore.

> "I am the good shepherd; and I know My sheep, and am known by my own. As the Father knows me, even so I know the Father; and lay down My life for the sheep."
> - John 10:14-15

Rainbow

Not long ago, I was driving home from a city nearby when I came upon a sight that was surreal. I remember it well, because I was just coming over the top of a hill in beautiful weather, and about a mile in front of me loomed a storm. It didn't cover the entire horizon.

Left to right, I could actually see the beginning and ending edges of the storm's width, and the road I was driving was a corridor through the middle. It was like I was about to drive into a picture. I could see the dark clouds and rain, but what really caught my eye was the rainbow! It was a complete rainbow and was on the side closest to me. How awesome! It was, at times, like these that I wish I could paint.

I got closer, and the clear skies above me grew gray, and the rain began. As I drove under the clouds and entered into the storm, any glimpse of the rainbow and the clear sky was gone, but I knew it was up there just out of my sight. It was as if there was a special secret between God and me. The cars headed my way had no idea of the beauty they would see at the end of the rain, but I did. Only when they saw the light after the storm would they see the rainbow.

The picture I had been given before I drove into the storm provided me with an insight that the others didn't have, and while I drove through the rain, I knew it would be short-lived for them. I was thankful for the lesson God gave me.

NEED A PROMISE?

Everyone is looking for a rainbow. Not literally, but figuratively. A promise, a pot of gold or light at the end of the tunnel. Many of us look for a picture-perfect solution to a less than perfect situation. I wonder, though, if we know what we really need. Sometimes what we think is a good answer is not an answer at all.

Dear God, I am in awe of the work of Your Hands and the majesty of this earth. Thank You for the rainbow, the sign of a promise between You and man. Your promise never fails, and for that, I am so grateful. Thank You for reminding me that even when I am under the clouds of a rainstorm, You are there above me and have the end in sight. Even though I can't have Your point of view, it is enough that You promise to see me through until I can see the sunshine again.

> "The rainbow shall be in the cloud, and I will look on it to remember the everlasting covenant between God and every living creature of all flesh that is on the earth."
>
> - Genesis 9:16

Raindrops

The other day I was driving during a sudden summer downpour. The rain was coming down in buckets so heavy that I could hardly see to drive. When I came to a stop at the traffic light, I sat there looking out the driver's window at the rain. Looking at it from the side view while I was stopped, it didn't seem quite so heavy.

It was still coming down hard, and I observed the raindrops hitting the pavement. It looked like they were hurling themselves to the earth like they were in a race. I could see the pattern as the large drops splatted, seemingly in a hurry to get somewhere.

As the light turned green and I drove on, I found myself in thought about them. It did seem like they were all quickly trying to go somewhere — and they would. They all hit the pavement; the water pooled into runoff and streamed quickly down the street. They all wound up somewhere together in a storm gutter or stream. In the end, all those drops were at the same place at the same time. It didn't matter when they had landed, or which one hit the pavement first.

It reminded me of man. So often, we hurl ourselves headlong into our day, into life, into a decision. We are at odds and competition with our fellow man and even ourselves. All of us headed somewhere. The thing is, we all started at the same place like the rain; we began from the heavens, and in the end, we all have a final destination. The journey in-between really counts and can impact so many lives. With the rain, as the drops fall from the sky, they are not at odds with each other.

They are not worried about overtaking each other or how fast they will reach the ground. It is the harmony and movement of millions of them together that create a life-giving rain shower. The unison of the drops paints a very powerful illustration; the force of a million little things heading in one direction can sustain life. The truth is that all of us on the same path, no matter how small, and when collectively focused on our final destination, can offer life-giving power for those who choose to believe.

STAYING DRY?

Isn't it sad that somehow in the midst of life, no matter what phase we are in, we don't always relish the experience we are gaining? Kids can't wait until their next birthday when they will be one number older. Teens tick off high school years in anticipation of graduation. Young adults are anxious to attend college or get a job and move out on their own. All of this is done as if it's a race.

It would be nice if the sense of hurry was replaced with a fluid sense of harmony like the raindrops . . . all going somewhere together, each small person contributing to the collective's bigger purpose, each in their own destined time

— still moving forward, pressing on for the prize — but each seeking the way as God has purposed, and each of us treasuring and marking the times between where we start and where we end.

Dear Heavenly Father, thank You for the rain, both literally and figuratively. The rain promotes growth. Lord, help me embrace it instead of running as quickly as I can to get back to a dry place. Instead, let me yield to You and focus on the life-giving power that only rain can give.

Help me to slow down and go into each day looking for You in the things that happen. Let me learn during the rain of unpleasant lessons, with the understanding that You are my safe harbor and that all rain ends. Help me remember that while I am getting wet, it means I can grow.

> "Not that I have already attained, or am already perfected; but I press on, that I may lay hold of that for which Christ Jesus has also laid hold of me. Brethren, I do not count myself to have apprehended; but one thing I do, forgetting those things which are behind and reaching forward to those things which are ahead, I press toward the goal for the prize of the upward call of God in Christ Jesus.
>
> Therefore, let us, as many as are mature, have this mind; and if in anything you think otherwise, God will reveal even this to you. Nevertheless, to the degree that we have already attained, let us walk by the same rule, let us be of the same mind." -Philippians 3:12-16

Road Trip

On New Year's Day, my daughter and I were out of state on vacation, visiting my son and his young family. The weather was cold, near freezing, with snow still in patches all over the ground. The light rain was turning into snow again, which was not good weather for any outdoor recreation. We'd been cooped up in the house for days and had cabin fever. My son and his wife needed to pick up something in Tulsa, about an hour and a half away, so we packed up and headed out.

I was seated in the second row of their SUV by my two-year-old granddaughter, and a short time into the trip, I watched her use her little feet one at a time to pry her boots off. She pulled up one foot, then the other, stretching her socks until they pulled off. Next, she took her little blanket and rearranged it to cover her legs and bare feet and snuggled down. Mission accomplished. Then she asked her mom (only her mom knew what she said) for her phone. My daughter-in-law handed it back, and I watched her play with her mom's cell phone. I continued watching as she tapped the movie store icon. When the movie store came up, she started scrolling until she got to the kids' section and started scrolling there. She found what she wanted and tapped the video to life. When it froze, she refused to hand it to anyone but her mother to get it going again, then her mom handed it back.

I saw how she held the phone and how perfectly it fit into her small hands. I could see her bright eyes watching every move on the screen in front of her.

Amazing, I thought to myself, at the incredible mind of this two-year-old little girl. I had a thought, and as quickly as it went across my mind, it flew out my mouth: "I'll bet that kids are super intelligent when they are born, knowing everything, and we train them to be dumb." Everyone laughed at the random thought.

Kids grow, learn and become molded into little people with their own thoughts, personalities, likes, and dislikes. But when young, they take it by faith — everything, they take by faith, and they hope for things so easily. They believe in the people and the things around them with wide-eyed innocence. They have a spirit of joy and laugh for hours on end. You see, the children count on someone bigger than themselves. They depend on the love, care, and concern of their parents and family, and they act on it. They find comfort, solace, and even peace in the arms of the people that love them.

Unfortunately, it is something that we learn to let go of as adults. We learn that people will disappoint us at some point, even parents because they are human. So, we learn to let go of our child-like ways as we grow older and forget how to depend on someone bigger than ourselves. In short, we lose faith. Without faith in something bigger than ourselves, where is the hope for us?

Having the eyes of a child to see the world as a different place than those around us can be a wonderful thing! To lock into the hope of trusting that someone bigger than ourselves is in charge. What a deep sleep we can have with that thought. We can wake up with laughter! This isn't flawed thinking; it is right thinking! Trust in someone bigger than yourself — trust in God.

This is not about being unrealistic or irresponsible; it is about finding the faith of a child to meet your Heavenly Father, who is willing to be your Daddy from now into eternity. Believing in something you can't see is what faith is all about. We work all week to earn a paycheck we haven't yet seen but believe it will come. We turn on switches believing that the electric company will provide. We turn on faucets and believe we'll get water.

Truly, there is no promise. Our faith in those things is flawed. We have simply learned to trust those things. For some reason, people don't have a hard time believing in man-made promises or things, but when it comes to God, it is a hard sell. Really, it's about choice. As for me, I would rather believe in the eternal promises of God —the God who rained manna from heaven and provided a river flow of water from a rock to supply for His children. Now that is something to believe in . . . a never-ending source and supply!

MAKE A REQUEST?

Abba Father. Daddy God.

The words used to describe an intimate relationship. Does it seem irreverent to you to call upon Him that way? I used to feel guilty asking God for simple things or things I desired.

Sometimes it seems so petty in comparison to the dire requests, the life, and death requests, made by desperate people.

Daily provision is a given to my children; they count on being able to have a meal and sleep in a bed. Yet, they have no shame in easily asking for their hearts' desire from me. It makes me think of a child in a theme park while walking along eating one of those giant, round, colorful lollipops. No kid really needs one of those, we all know it, but as parents, we buy it for them anyway.

Why would our God, our Heavenly Father, feel differently than that towards us, His own children? He is able, but we can't feel ashamed for asking, no matter the size of the request. He knows our thoughts and intent of heart anyway, so why not just talk about it with Him?

Father God, as your child, I pray to You. Like any child talking to a parent asking for something, I wait to hear back. I need answers. Father, teach me to listen for Your voice. I know that You can speak to my heart, but I must learn to listen. Father, let me realize more and more each day that the answers to my prayers are found in Your Word. Just like a parent's words and advice come back to a child when they need them, Your words were established and are forever fixed to be my guideposts. Help me to read Your Word and put it in my heart, so it rings in my mind when I need it and find the answers to my prayers You gave me so long ago.

"Assuredly, I say to you, whoever does not receive the kingdom of God as a little child will by no means enter it."

-Luke 18:17

"Ask, and it will be given to you; seek, and you will find; knock, and it will be opened to you. For everyone who asks receives, and he who seeks finds, and to him who knocks it will be opened. Or what man is there among you who, if his son asks for bread, will give him a stone? Or if he asks for a fish, will he give him a serpent? If you then, being evil, know how to give good gifts to your children, how much more will your Father who is in heaven give good things to those who ask Him!" -Matthew 7:7-11

Road Signs

*H*ave you ever *lived* somewhere where road construction never seems to end? It is frustrating when you have to go through it in high traffic. As I drove to work today, there was yet more construction starting when the old wasn't even complete. It was now one giant construction zone. There were lots of signs about work ahead. There was one sign that said, "Exit Closed," and another sign that signaled a curve in the road. There were orange barrels on the right-hand side of the highway blocking off exits. At one blocked-off exit, there was an orange sign that said "Power Lines", and a big black arrow pointing up. There were also signs that said "slow, road work". All of this was to get one job accomplished.

Construction is a type of work that has to be done for improvement, for progress. What would modern-day travel be like if all roads were still dirt roads? It takes a plan, patience, and work to get new roads, but in the end, it is a better thing for us. Typically, we don't like delays and inconvenience.

I wonder what it would be like if we had directional signs in our lives to let us know when there's road work ahead. I thought about what people do when there is construction going on — they avoid it. Instead of taking their normal route, they detour. Perhaps that is why we aren't given a road map for our life. If we could see life and what was coming ahead, we'd take wrong exits, switch lanes and take detours to avoid the road work and construction delays.

That is how we should see the potholes of our life and work that has to be done. It is not always pleasant or an easy process when there is a need for change and growth, but it is necessary. If we could avoid it, progress would never take place.

IS IT A SIGN?

Are you paying attention to the road signs in your life? Do you take the curves with faith, knowing that even though you can't see the road, God will keep you on track? We should pay attention while driving through the construction zones, knowing they require extra care, and at times, slow down and pay attention to what the signs say, knowing that they are speaking with a good reason that we don't yet see. We should trust God when an exit is closed; it is for our eventual progress.

Lord, I am grateful that I don't know all that lies ahead of me. If I did, I would avoid all of the unpleasant things and choose the easiest path. I know from experience that the easiest is not always what is best. It takes time, lessons, and work to build faith and character. Lord, as I go through my life, enlighten me. Show me when I am in the construction phases of my life and help me to pay attention while I am passing through. Let me remember that You are the power line overhead to which I have access all of the time. Help me to recognize the lanes, exits, and shoulders; keep me on a route designed by You for my plans.

> "In all your ways acknowledge Him, And He shall direct your paths." -Proverbs 3:6

Roly-Polies

The other day, my daughter and I went looking for roly-polies. We were successful and found several of them at the edge of a nearby flowerbed. When we moved the rock, and they began to crawl away, my daughter looked at them, asking why they were called roly-polies. I touched one of the bugs, and it curled into a ball. She smiled and touched one herself. "You poke them, and they curl up!" I smiled back at her, and we went back to the roly-polies.

As I watched them, I realized that people are like roly-polies. If people poke at us emotionally, we curl up and shut them out almost immediately. To paraphrase my beloved pastor, "When temptation and trials come, when someone says something or does something to offend you, it is your opportunity. God is watching to see if you come out of the character of Christ." I was reminded of an incident I'd had recently regarding a school crossing guard.

In our town, the crossing guards seem to have some policy; they pass out big waves and smiles to all the people who drive by. Recently, a new guard appeared at my daughter's school.

She didn't seem to know the policy. In fact, you don't even see a smile on her. I thought I'd be kind and start by waving first.

I gave a full-wave, and she gave back a half-wave. Okay, I thought. I skipped a few days, and then I gave her a mild wave, to which she started to respond but stopped. A couple of days later, I drove past and found myself muttering, "Well, okay, don't wave!" I became a little indignant over a non-waving crossing guard. How silly of me.

My pastor's words came to mind, and I felt ashamed. I started something she didn't ask for anyway. God spoke to my heart; I had no idea of who she was or what trials she was going through. Yet with one "poke," I'd curled up and shut her out instead of continuing to be friendly. You know, roly-polies can't go anywhere as long as they stay curled up.

WHAT'S BUGGING YOU?

Is there someone or something that's got you balled up inside, something that has you all tied up? If something is bugging you, exterminate it with love.

Lord, I ask that You keep my feet walking in love. Remind me that love always finds a way through. Love doesn't shut down after being provoked. Love is patient, and love is kind. When I am provoked, *that* is when I should begin to walk in Your love. I am so grateful to You, Father, that You are not easily offended. If You were, You would have closed off the heavens to me long ago. Thank You for Your patience with me, God. Help me to have the same patience You show towards us when I deal with others, and not close off those who have offended me. It is my opportunity to show Your love.

> "When I was a child, I spoke as a child, I understood as a child; but when I became a man, I put away childish things. For now, we see in a mirror, dimly, but then face-to-face. Now I know in part, but then I shall know just as I also am known. And now abide faith, hope, love, these three, but the greatest of these is love." -1 Corinthians 13:11-13

Square Peg, Round Hole

Growing up, I used to watch a PBS kids TV show that used a skit with a song, "One of these things is not like the others; one of these things just doesn't belong." That was the only thing that came to my mind recently when I was at work, my third week at a new job. I was at a small-town school where I was an entry-level cook after retiring from my last job of twenty-three years. Everyone in the complex knew each other, and if the walls could talk, I was certain they would bear the secrets of everyone who had ever walked the halls.

I never saw the movie, so I don't know why, but the words of the Harper Valley PTA song came to mind. Every day, each time I went through the kitchen, I saw a different pair of people whispering. I felt like a target. Nobody knew my level of expertise, nor did they care. This particular day, I was a square peg trying to get into a round hole; I was angry, and I was done. Couldn't these people see what I offered them if they let me in?

Frustrated, I left out the back door to take out the trash and vent to myself. As I walked, I wanted to swear so badly that I barely stopped the words as they began to fall out of my open mouth. You see, the devil always likes to get ahold of me about something that I don't like in anyone else and rarely have done — cursing. Instead of speaking my mind, my heart took over, and I heard God's Word in the matter.

The Word of God I'd read earlier that week stopped the mental freight train I was on, which could have wrecked my Christian witness. As I walked back towards the kitchen door and began to get right, the truth struck me. I realized that I *was* a square peg trying to fit in a round hole, that I *am* different, and God intends it to be that way. Not being like others, not responding in kind, but instead allowing myself to be used as salt and light was the whole point.

Once again, I recalled the words of a dear friend advising me to stay in the character of Christ. If it wasn't for keeping God's Word in front of my eyes on a daily basis, even in the smallest way, I might have missed it that day. Sometimes our jobs can get in the way of the work we are called to do, God's work, if we let it. Today, God saved me from myself, and I went back inside with my secret victory. I dropped the offense and embraced the work.

NOT A FIT?

Sometimes we just don't feel like a fit. We don't feel like the right fit for a certain person, job, or solution. However, our feelings don't always matter. There are times when God's idea of what fits prevails. When we are picked by Him, and He places us in a person's life, a job, or to be a solution for something... at those times, when we know God is in charge, we yield ourselves to Him.

The next time you feel like you don't fit the plan, maybe instead, you should ask Him if you were hand-picked for the job. God needs square pegs.

Dear Heavenly Father, I am so glad that I get to be a part of something bigger than myself; I get to be a part of the Kingdom's calling. I'm thankful You allow me to be a part of Your body here on earth, reaching out to those around me. It is my prayer, Lord, that when I come before You, the shadow of the Cross covers me with mercy and grace that is only Yours to give, and I am forgiven. Likewise, let me always forgive those around me, so You get the glory. Amen.

> "You are the salt of the earth; but if the salt loses its flavor, how shall it be seasoned? It is then good for nothing but to be thrown out and trampled underfoot by men. You are the light of the world. A city that is set on a hill cannot be hidden. Nor do they light a lamp and put it under a basket, but on a lampstand, and it gives light to all who are in the house. Let your light so shine before men, that they may see your good works and glorify your Father in heaven."
> -Matthew 5:13-16

> "With the tongue we praise our Lord and Father, and with it we curse human beings, who have been made in God's likeness. Out of the same mouth come praise and cursing. My brothers and sisters, this should not be."
> -James 3:9-10 NIV

Shipping and Receiving

Seeds are a funny thing. I'm not talking about seeds from a package that grows plants. I am talking about seeds of wisdom. They're planted, waiting to drop a golden nugget into your spirit once the seed germinates and the truth comes forth. People drop seeds into our minds all of our lives. Many times, we don't even recognize that it has happened. It may be through a conversation, a book, the internet, or an email, but they come. You don't get it right away, but then one day, the seed cracks open right when you need it — the epiphany, that golden nugget - drops right into your heart and mind, taking you to a new level of spiritual wisdom. Germination can be quick or a long time coming.

My most recent experience was in the middle of the night after a phone call from my friend, Maggie, the night before. During the phone conversation, Maggie found out that I had recently driven myself to the ER late one night when I was in distress. She told me that the next time I should call her, and she would go with me. She kindly told me that I wasn't the lone ranger and that I should drop off pride.

She also said that when people are physically hurting and a doctor brings a seriously negative report, sometimes they can't reject it by themselves, and it is good to have someone there with you who can. It made sense, so I agreed, citing there wouldn't be a next time anytime soon. Then at 3:47 A.M., as I was rolling over in bed, God watered, and the seed she had sown cracked.

As I started to roll over, my left shoulder pained me something fierce, and I thought to myself, well, you are getting older, and arthritis runs in our family . . . so on and so forth. And in the middle of that conversation with myself about why I hurt, God interrupted and dropped it in — that's because I choose to believe it. Just Like That. I realized that *the moment we mentally accept something is the moment we own it, and it becomes our truth.* God is awesome like that in the middle of the night!

Most people have experienced delivery trucks coming and leaving packages. When a delivery comes to a business, it has to be checked in, and someone signs for what is on the truck. Same for small packages; that is so that there is a receiving record for accountability — likewise, with us and our minds. When we mentally accept a bad health report, resign ourselves to things others have said about us or accept myths, we have signed on the dotted line. At that point, we have received it for ourselves as the truth. The problem is that once we accept something with our hearts and minds, we can't just wrap it up and send it back as easily as a physical delivery. Once we have accepted something into our spirit like that, it must be plucked out by the root. We have to denounce it out loud. Then we must affirm the truth, a scripture to the contrary that states God's truth in the matter until it becomes so ingrained that we can't even think upon anything else.

POINT OF ORIGIN?

All people ship with their words; as Christians, we should guard the seeds we are sending out. And most definitely, don't be shipping out or receiving anything into your mind if it doesn't reflect God's word in the matter! Rejecting on the spot is so much better than trying to return something received in error.

Dear God, thank You for the power of choice. I need to carefully choose the reports that I will believe. Remind me that my faith in You and Your promises supersede all other things. Let me search the Bible for promises to believe in and to count on, not looking to earthly things. Let my mind be stayed on You, God, as it says in Isaiah, "Who has believed our report? And to whom has the arm of the Lord been revealed?"

> "Finally, brethren, whatever things are true, whatever things are noble, whatever things are just, whatever things are pure, whatever things are lovely, whatever things are of good report, if there is any virtue and if there is anything praiseworthy—meditate on these things." -Philippians 4:8

Signs of Life

My daughter received a peace lily plant from a family friend, and I helped her care for the plant. It grew and quickly needed repotting, so I did that. It had to move from inside the house, outside onto the back patio. It didn't do too well on the back patio, so I decided to move it to our front porch where there was more shade and not too much noon sun.

One morning when I went out to care for it, it was chewed down to nubs. We lived on the outskirts of town, and deer were known to cruise through our neighborhood, and I realized what had happened. The peace lily had been somebody's meal. I thought the plant might come back, so I kept tending to it.

We moved, a temporary move, and took the plant with us. A year later, when our permanent housing situation two states away came up, I realized that the plant was dead. It made me sad because the plant was sentimental to us. Still, it made no sense to carry a pot of dirt with sticks in it all that way, so I pulled up the root ball and headed to the garbage can across the yard. As I lifted the lid and started to toss the plant in, something caught my eye.

Deep in those dead sticks, I saw a tinge of green. I took the root ball and looked a bit closer. Yes, there were one or two tiny green sprigs in there. It excited me to see a sign of life in there! I just couldn't throw it away now. It went back into the pot, was watered, and hauled across two states to move.

At our new home, I continued to water the sticks and watch over it. Lo and behold, it continued to have new growth sprouts. Weeks and months went by, and it started looking like a normal plant again. It was a little hard to understand because the care of the plant hadn't really changed, yet it was now growing.

Over the winter, I moved it into the garage, keeping it warm and watered, and by early summer, there was a thriving, large, blooming peace lily! It was hard to believe. What was once thought dead had come roaring back to life. It reminded me of something God had shown me spiritually; He is a resurrection God. He is the God of another chance, of healing and of restoration. Much like He did with the plant, He can do for us in our lives over situations with insurmountable odds.

He is able.

DEAD ROOTS?

Have you ever just given up hope on something that you thought would never work or had an idea that you just couldn't see through to fruition? Sometimes, there are things we just can't seem to do on our own, but God can enable us if we call on Him. Before putting a plan to rest in the trash heap, look deep inside and call on God. You might see signs of life once again.

God, I thank You for resurrection life. You raised Lazarus, You raised Jesus, and You healed lepers and caused the blind to see. You multiplied fishes and loaves and walked on water. You are near to the brokenhearted. Lord, if it is broken, remind me to give it to You and let You work.

> "The Lord is my shepherd; I shall not want. He makes me to lie down in green pastures; He leads me beside the still waters. He restores my soul; He leads me in the paths of righteousness for His name's sake." -Psalm 23:1-3

Sunflowers

By the side of the road, on a grassy slope near my home, stands a patch of sunflower stalks. I frequently pass them on my drive to work. Personally, I'm not a big fan of yellow flowers, but these were just beautiful — their flower faces turned upward towards the sun. The plants stood so tall and straight; it looked as if the roots were digging into the ground, and they were stretching hard towards the sky. The proud-looking flower stalks stood out from the rest on the side of the road. I knew that they were seeking the sun. Actually, they were basking in the sun. I knew that as the sun moved through the sky as the day wore on, the sunflowers would bend following its direction.

    I recalled seeing this before with other plants. I'd seen entire groups of plants bowing towards the sunlight. I'd also seen how my indoor plants act when they are close to a window where there's light. The plant stretches towards the light. Sunlight is the life source of the plant, and it knows it may die without it. The plants revel in worshiping the sun and flourish because of it. The relationship between the two is evident and beautiful for all to see, the plant and the life source. There is nothing seen between the two of them but blue sky, but there is a definite connection that is easy to see.

Nature is not shy.

The thoughts almost embarrassed me as I thought about showing the connection between my Maker and me. I have the opportunity every day to make my stance toward the Son known, but I am sure that there are times when it can't be seen by those around me. The truth is, just like I became familiar with the sunflowers and grew fond of the yellow as I watched them grow through the weeks, so it is with people. We think we lead private lives, but our faces display what is inside us for others to see; our lives and roots are revealed to onlookers who pay attention.

The root which holds us connects us to life. If I was to go and cut the sunflowers and put them in a vase, they would begin to die the moment they were severed from the stalk of the plant. I wouldn't see it right away, but the moment they are cut apart, the flowers have no hope of surviving. The relationship I saw in nature caused me to think and to pray.

ARE YOU ROOTED?

We all have roots — the people and things who shape us, influence us, feed our soul. God gives our spirit life. Just like the sunflower will die if cut from the root, so will our faith if we separate ourselves from Christ. We have to read His Word to water our spirit, so our root is never separated from Him. He is the Light that sustains all life.

Dear Heavenly Father, teach me to worship You in a way like the plants worship the sun. Help me to dig down and plant my roots firmly and stand tall for You as I look for You each day. Let my face shine towards You and put me in remembrance that You are my life source. Let me follow You throughout the course of my day and bow towards You. Let my seeking You be on display for all to see and cause them to look towards Your Light.

> "For the Lord God is a sun and shield: The Lord will give grace and glory: No good thing will He withhold from them that walk uprightly." -Psalm 84:11

> "For I am persuaded that neither death nor life, nor angels nor principalities nor powers, nor things present nor things to come, nor height nor depth, nor any other created thing, shall be able to separate us from the love of God which is in Christ Jesus our Lord." -Romans 8:38-39

Sunlight

My *daughter attends an* elementary school near our house. To get to the school, I go through our neighborhood, and at a four-way stop at the end of our block, I turn left. Almost immediately after, I make a right turn into a long, steep driveway that takes me to the front school entrance. It was only after arriving at the entrance for the first time, where the driveway levels off in front of the school, that I realized the breathtaking vantage point of this hill.

As I left the school, turning the curve in the long, horseshoe-shaped drive to exit, I looked to the left on the valley of houses I'd driven through to get here, and the opposing hill on the other side — beautiful. Some days, I just sit there in my van at the end of the horseshoe drive as long as I can and take it in. The view is like a picture when the morning sun rises, and the houses nestled on the opposing hillside begin peeking out of the shadows as the sunlight casts on them. The houses at the top gleam brilliantly in the sun, and the ones below them will be next to shine. As the morning sun rises, the houses are sequentially covered in light.

I remember one morning it struck me so much that I just followed that line of thought as I drove to work. I saw the school's football field stadium seating. At the top, the aluminum seats were shining so bright it was near blinding, but the ones below were still waiting for the sun to climb high enough to shine on them. As I drove through neighborhoods, I noticed the early morning light pouring through the trees, creating a warm glow through the autumn leaves.

By noon that day, the sun was high in the baby-blue sky, and everything below received the same bright light on it. The only thing that changed how the sun rested on objects was if something got in the way of the light. It could be a puff of cloud or telephone pole casting a shadow. Perhaps just the position of how the object was sitting in the sun. The sun was shining on everything, and it reminded me of God's love.

God's love is there for all of us. It is unhampered and shines on all. There may be objects that get in the way of His love falling on us, objects we allow or put there, but His love is waiting for a clearing to shine on us. We have to be looking towards God, facing Him, to see His brightness. Nevertheless, when it is dark outside, the sun is still in the sky even though we can't see it. When our lives are dark, God is still there; we just have to wait for the time when we can see Him clearly again.

NOON SUN

As my five-year-old granddaughter would say, "Here's the deal." God doesn't care about our position. He doesn't care on which level of the stadium seating we are sitting in.

Our position doesn't affect His ability because His position is always the same. However, our position can decide how we receive it. For full effect, I would face the Son.

Heavenly Father, in times of darkness, let me remember there is light, even if I can't see it. Help me to feel Your warmth around me and look for the Son. I know that Jesus came to give us life and give it more abundantly, and that means being able to withstand the wiles of the enemy and face dark places in life. I ask You to be the warmth in my heart, the light in my dark day. Help me to remember that the Son is always there even when I can't feel Him, and days will become brighter as Your love causes the darkness to fade away.

> "But for you who revere my name, the sun of righteousness will rise with healing in its rays. And you will go out and frolic like well-fed calves." -Malachi 4:2 NIV

The One Person

There have been *many* times in my life where one person — *just one* — made a significant impact on my life. As a young adult, I'd taken the GED, ACT, and moved two hundred fifty miles away from family to attend college.

It had been a struggle for nearly two years. This time I only had a few months to go, but things had piled up to what seemed insurmountable odds to finish this course in my life. I stood there in the glassed office building, near the pool of my apartment complex. I was embarrassed, choking back tears while explaining my situation to the apartment manager. It was the first of the month, and I only had one-third of the rent due. I finished my story by telling the manager I was so tired of struggling, and I was just going to quit school; it was my only choice.

The manager sat up tall in her chair, and with all the strength in her voice she could muster without shouting, she said, "Don't quit. You cannot quit. Promise me you won't." She then explained that in her youth, she had a scholarship, which she had to give up. It hurt her, and she never forgot that incomplete part of her life. She translated that story into an urgency on my behalf to finish what I'd started.

She explained she would do everything she could on her end to keep my apartment, just pay her what I could and tell her what was going on.

With each encouraging, brave word she spoke, my spirit found enough strength to think maybe, just maybe, I could still do this. Six months later, I walked the stage and got my diploma during the first summer graduation ever held in the thirty-nine years of that college. One person — *just one person* — altered my path of what might have been.

Yet another time while in college, right before my last finals, I got conjunctivitis so bad, my eyes were as red as a bullfighter's cape. I went to the E.R. and got some medical help. I slept on the couch and rested for one afternoon, and the next day I got up to attend classes. Downstairs, ready to go, my car wouldn't start. With my final speech due and no other options, I got out of the car and headed on foot to the nearest bus stop. I was overwhelmed and feeling pitiful. I took a seat, and at the opposite end of the covered bench was a can. It was an empty Campbell's soup can with the end of a spoon sticking out the top. Obviously, it had been someone's meal.

I adjusted my mood a little. I saw writing on the can, and thinking it might be some desperate plea for help, I picked it up to read. These were the words I found: "God so loved the world, He gave His only begotten Son, and whosoever believeth in Him, shall not perish but have everlasting life."

My stomach caved like a deep pit. Someone — *one person* — with so little means left a message of hope for me to see. I reeled with guilt. A couple of blocks away, I had an apartment with electricity, cool air, cable tv, and all the comforts of home. I had no right to feel any kind of way but grateful. That *one person* saved me from myself, and I launched into my day head-on, no longer feeling pitiful or overwhelmed. I was okay, and I'd be okay. I prayed for the person who left that message on the can.

Last, but not least, there is Elena. Elena was my caregiver for many years while my parents managed their business at night. In fact, young Elena lived with us. One night while she was deeply entrenched in T.V., refusing to give me the attention only a bored eight-year-old could demand, I told her I was lonely. As I sulked nearby, dwarfed in my father's overstuffed, brown leather recliner, I explained to her that I had no friends or anyone to talk to. She stopped, shifting her eyes and attention to me, and said, "You're never alone. Jesus is with you; talk to Him."

When I asked her how I could do that and why I couldn't see him, she explained it sufficiently, and I began talking to God as if He were an invisible friend, which He was! I don't think I've ever stopped. But because of one person, just one person —Elena — I began communicating with God, and He met me where I was at in my young faith. As time went on, I learned the gentle nudge of the heart and mind that belong only to Him, and I am forever grateful.

God showed me that you don't know when *you* are somebody's one person; when you are the one word of hope, the one voice of wisdom, the one encourager, the one act of kindness, the one helping hand, the one light in the dark, the one opportunity to introduce them to hope in Christ!

ARE YOU THE ONE?

You are the impact on somebody's life. Maybe more than one somebody. You might not even know it when it happens. You might not realize the impact you make as a friend, employee, mom, husband, wife, classmate, volunteer, or someone just paying it forward.

But your actions and words matter. They may bring hope to the hopeless or joy to the joyless. They may inspire, lead and serve people in every walk of life. You have a voice, and even your silence speaks. We should all understand the importance of our words and whether they give light or darkness; they will land and have an impact whether we mean it or not. We can choose to speak life-giving, light-filled words so when they land, they provide cover to those in need.

Lord Jesus, thank You for all the times You hold me when I feel down. Thank You for Your presence when I feel alone. You are always there at what I think will be the bottom, waiting to hold me, to catch me. Lord, let me share that with others in need. Allow me to share Your Word with them so they can feel You holding them, just like You always do for me. Your Word causes wellsprings of hope in us, Lord, and I thank You for Your never-ending supply.

> "Then the King will say to those on His right hand, 'Come, you blessed of My Father, inherit the kingdom prepared for you from the foundation of the world: for I was hungry and you gave Me food; I was thirsty and you gave Me drink; I was a

stranger and you took Me in; I was naked and you clothed Me; I was sick and you visited Me; I was in prison and you came to Me.'

"Then the righteous will answer Him, saying, 'Lord, when did we see You hungry and feed You, or thirsty and give You drink? When did we see You a stranger and take You in, or naked and clothe You? Or when did we see You sick, or in prison, and come to You?' And the King will answer and say to them, 'Assuredly, I say to you, inasmuch as you did it to one of the least of these My brethren, you did it to Me.'"
-Matthew 25:34-40

"There is one body and one spirit, just as you were called in one hope of your calling; one Lord, one faith, one baptism; one God and Father of all, who is above all, and through all, and in you all." -Ephesians 4:4-6

Traffic Jam

When you work as a restaurant manager, you don't punch a time clock. The day is at least ten hours long, if not fourteen. So, when I purposed to leave for the day by five-thirty and get home to see my daughter before church friends took her to an "away" football game, it was important to me. I left work and entered the expressway. I was switching into the left lane, getting into full speed, when the traffic came to an abrupt halt.

I looked to the right behind me, quickly trying to switch back to the other lane so I could take the exit next to me, but no. The traffic was steady and coming quickly. I knew escape was only one lane over through the exit. I looked all around, but nothing. In a moment's time, I was stuck. I called my daughter and told her what was going on and that I might not make it home to see her off. I gave her instructions on what to do, gave her my love, and hung up, hoping I'd still get home before she left.

Where I was on the road, I couldn't yet see how far the traffic jam lasted. We don't live in a metropolitan area, so traffic jams aren't expected. I wondered if it was an accident, construction lane closure, or something else holding up traffic. It took thirty minutes for me to travel the short distance from the exit I'd missed to the connecting overpass. At that point, against the dusk sky, red car taillights lit up the road as far as my eyes could see. UGH. I sat there wondering how I could make it home before my daughter left. I took a deep breath, resolute that it was going to be a while and that I would just have to see my daughter after the game.

I was stuck in the left lane beside the cement construction barricades that stretched for miles. With nowhere to go, I found myself studying it. I looked at the air holes in it, the places for water to drain through. I noticed the seams and the many reflectors. I took note of the round cement cylinders alongside the construction equipment in the median. These were all things that I wouldn't notice, going sixty miles per hour down the road. Then, I looked at the other people sitting in their cars around me. One lady had her window down, deliberately singing loudly off-key, drawing attention to herself.

There was a man who had been in the lane right next to me, who got frustrated and drove off into the grass, trying to cut through and find passage. Yet another lady I saw in her van was talking on her phone the entire hour as we crept along, her hand gestures showing she was aggravated.

I took the opportunity to look at things that could only be afforded to someone going at this slow pace. I even saw a three-inch-tall Bugs Bunny figurine sitting on top of the cement barricade, poised as if someone left it there for me to find. How funny . . . you never know what you will find in unexpected places. It then occurred to me that the entire situation had a spiritual parallel.

I was right where I was supposed to be. If my timing had been five seconds different when I first changed lanes entering the expressway, I'd have been able to exit, taking a different route home. And at first, I couldn't see what was going on ahead, so I even prayed for people in case it was an accident. This was not about me. It was about someone or something else. At my slowed pace, I was given the opportunity to stop and think, to pray for another, and to see things from a view not normally seen. This time I got it — the message of acceptance.

Acceptance. By staying quiet, I could hear God if He spoke to my heart, and by accepting my place, God could shift my focus to someone and something else besides my own inconvenience. By taking this time to look around, He could show me things that others would never know were there. The lady singing to bring attention to herself, the man who left the road so frustrated he took an illegal route, and the woman talking on the phone, would not get the same message I did. I don't think God leaves a message "at the tone." We have to be ready to hear Him and pick up the line, and I am glad that this time I was ready to answer.

IN A JAM?

Have you been in any jams? Ask yourself and God why you are in a jam and then open your heart to listen. You'll find your exit right past the lesson that is waiting to be learned.

Father God, thank You for the road in life that I am on. It is no mistake. Let me accept Your path for my life and open my eyes so that I don't take the wrong exit. It isn't always about my path, but about the lives of the others around me. Sometimes we have to stop in our path and be a part of what is going on around us, helping and praying for others in a time of need. It is about listening to the lady who is trying to call attention to herself; it is about helping someone not to be so frustrated that they do something illegal. Lord, it is about finding You in the midst of where we are and sharing You with others in need. Father, I accept that You are in charge and always right on time.

> "Trust in the Lord with all your heart, and lean not on your own understanding; in all your ways acknowledge Him, and He shall direct your paths." -Proverbs 3:5-6

Water Heater

Out of the blue, we began having water pressure problems in our house. Not the whole house, mind you, but only half of it, and not all of the water but only the hot. The master bathroom was the worst. The sink hot water and the shower hot water went down to a trickle. If you turned on the sink hot water while the shower was on, no water would come out of the shower and vice versa. To get it fixed, the landlords were called in to help.

They came to the house and determined it was the water heater and installed a new one for us, which required removing the door frame and re-installing it. It was an all-day job. In the end, the old water heater was full of sediment at the bottom, and we all thought for sure that once the new one was installed, the problem would be gone, but alas, it was not — the water still would not flow. They then blew out the lines with an air compressor, but that did not help either. The owners went home dismayed at the end of the day. We gave it a week or so of sharing one bathroom and giving the lines a chance to clear out. That didn't help either.

The next weekend came, and the landlords returned with their friend, the plumber. That, too, was an all-day job, and it stumped even the experienced plumber. One person manned the water heater with a compressor to blow the air, another person in the bathroom to holler back the results. When the plumber blew the line, the water pressure increased, but when he quit, the water pressure stopped. After several hours of working, he found the problem! It was a small marble from the old water heater that had broken free and found its way into the water line, lodging itself in a wall pipe near the water heater. Unbelievable!

A small white marble blocking the water to half of the house changed the way we lived for a week! Such a small thing was causing such a major problem causing even a professional a whole day to find it. That is how it is with us spiritually.

God does not block blessings from us, but sometimes we cause it ourselves by being in the wrong place. We can be in places, situations, relationships, or even jobs where we weren't meant to be, and nothing flows right for us or even goes bad. When God instructs us, directs us, tugs at us to do one thing, and we ignore it to do another, it can become the marble in our water line blocking the flow. Sometimes I believe we "get lost" in our own lives.

You might find yourself at a place where you can hardly feel connected to God anymore, like the flow of faith just isn't there. Maybe it is not you at all, but just in the wrong place. Much like the marble stopped the water, our own choices can put us in a place where there is an absence of peace, balance, and fulfillment. To get it fixed, you can't call a plumber. Instead, call on God and look for the answer.

HOW'S YOUR PRESSURE?

Sometimes we just need to be in the flow of things . . . when everything is going wrong, and we are walking upstream with the water rushing around our legs so hard that we are tired of standing in opposition to the flow. Sometimes we just want to drop, fall into the water flow, and let it take us away.

Actually, that is exactly what we should do — it is the answer. Close your eyes, take a deep breath, and exhale as you let go. Let everything go and fall into peace; fall into flow with the love of God and the Mercy of Christ. Let the problems flow out of our minds, leaving our cares at His feet.

God can put us in a new condition.

Lord, when the water of life is rising up around me, let Your Words be my rock and foundation, which keep my head above the waters. Let me remember to cast my cares upon You, for You care for me.

> "Do not be anxious about anything, but in every situation, by prayer and petition, with thanksgiving, present your requests to God. And the peace of God, which transcends all understanding, will guard your hearts and your minds in Christ Jesus." -Philippians 4:6-7 NIV

Water Towers

When I got into my car to go to work today, I sat in the driveway for a couple of minutes, making mirror adjustments. When I was done, I paused for a moment before I began to back out, looking over to the left. My line of vision went straight to the crest of the hill, at the end of our subdivision, several blocks away. On that crest, one after another in a horizontal row, was a cylinder-shaped water tower, a tree, and another tree. Both trees were the same size and about one third the height of the tower. Just the way they sat there in a row made me think that one day, they might all be the same height.

All the trees need is some water to grow. It occurred to me that the one thing that the trees need is right beside them. Then the irony of it played in my mind; the trees won't get one drop of water they need from that tower. They can't because they aren't tapped into it.

On the way to work, I saw other water towers, and I began counting them. There was a total of ten. The water towers are for supplying the surrounding areas. Unlike the trees, the homes, businesses, and other places can draw on the water within the towers. Although the supply lines are unseen, they are there underground, waiting to carry the water on demand. However, like the trees, it is possible that the homes or businesses might not get one drop of water from the towers either.

The relationship between the water and the houses is established by pipes, but the nature of the relationship is that the request has to be made from the house by turning on a water valve. If the valve for water is never turned on, then the water will never be received in that way. The water flow requires an action initiated by another. If there is a need for water, it will go unquenched if the valve isn't ever turned on. This is not unlike the spiritual relationship we have with God.

The relationship is already established. Man is God's creation made in His image. God is man's source and supply. But much like the relationship between the water tower and surrounding areas, there can be a need that will not be supplied unless a request is made to the source. Just like the supply of water goes untapped unless a valve is turned on, we have to turn on the valve that will open up the flow between ourselves and God. He is there waiting to be our source, but we must first call upon Him and learn to recognize His answers. God does not force Himself upon anyone; He wants to be invited in.

OPEN VALVES?

My nephew is a geologist. He loves all things of earth and sky. His expertise brought him to work within the oil industry, and he deals with the technology of equipment every day. He has a passion for it. He, for one, would tell you that there is much to be said for valves. A simplistic breakdown by my own standards? Open valves allow flow to happen, and closed valves prevent flow. Easy Peasy. If we have Jesus as the connection between ourselves and God, the valve is always open to the throne from where all blessings flow.

Lord, I am so glad that You are my source and supply. Unlike a tree unable to get water, You are able and willing to quench my thirst. All I have to do is ask You. I don't have to stay thirsty — no matter what it is that I need. Father, just as You rained manna from heaven and caused water to come forth from a rock to give Your people what they needed in times of old, so You still supply our needs. Your Word says that You are the same yesterday, today, and forever. I am forever grateful, and I open up the lines between us with prayer.

> "Jesus answered and said to her, "If you knew the gift of God, and who it is who says to you, 'Give Me a drink,' you would have asked Him, and He would have given you living water." The woman said to Him, "Sir, You have nothing to draw with, and the well is deep. Where then do You get that living water? Are You greater than our father Jacob, who gave us the well, and drank from it himself, as well as his sons and his livestock?"
>
> Jesus answered and said to her, "Whoever drinks of this water will thirst again, but whoever drinks of the water that I shall give him will never thirst. But the water that I shall give him will become in him a fountain of water springing up into everlasting life." -John 4: 10-14

Weeds and Seeds

Have you ever noticed that weeds seem to grow anywhere? All they need is a spot of dirt to take hold.

Outside the back door where I work, there is a four-foot-tall growth of some kind that spouted from where the concrete wall meets the asphalt ground. There is nothing around it but asphalt and cement, yet it appears to thrive.

I have seen this in other places too. Little purple flowers and creeping green plants dot sidewalk cracks wherever there is a bit of room for them to sprout. The same thing goes at my house. I have to go out and work the flowerbed to keep the weeds to a minimum. The weeds grow regardless of the soil condition, rain, or drought. They need no care to grow. Yet for seeds that I have planted or new plants that I have bought and planted, I must take special care so that they grow and don't die. I use fertilizer, water and guard them. Then, with the right combination of care, they will flourish.

The stark distinction between the weeds and my plants brings me to God.

NEED A GARDENER?

I love the beautiful gardens of the mansion grounds seen in movies — the houses filled with fresh cuts of greenery and flowers. They make it seem so stately, so grandiose. In real life, not many of us can go out and collect beauty like that from our own yards, but we do grow a bounty in our heart.

What's more, the Bible says that our mouth speaks from the abundance of the heart, which is difficult to cultivate, as weed pulling is a never-ending process. So, make it easy on yourself and ask for help. The Master Gardener will come in and till the ground, sow the seed and water with His Word. After all, gardens are part of His creation.

Lord, I give You my heart. Come and be the gardener and till the ground within, plant in me seeds of Your Word — words of hope, wisdom, light, and life.

Let the ground of my heart be good ground, not choked out by the weeds or cares of this world. Let Your Word be the root within me that will never be plucked out. Lord, make it that no matter how barren it may look, there is always another seed there waiting to germinate, to flourish, and bring forward bounty enough to share.

> "Having been born again, not of corruptible seed but incorruptible, through the word of God which lives and abides forever, because All flesh is as grass, And all the glory of man as the flower of the grass. The grass withers, and its flower falls away, but the word of the Lord endures forever."
>
> -1 Peter 1:23-25

Still On The Road...

On the same trip to Waco that day, where I saw the fog in the distance, there were many other things I noticed as I went down the road. I saw sunflowers with their roots dug into the ground, their faces turned, stretching towards the sky. I noticed overpasses where grass and flowers were sprouting out from cracks in the cement. I noticed the trees along the roadside and an occasional farm or ranch . . . and signs — lots and lots of signs. Here I was in my car alone, driving past all of these things that were behind me quick as a flash. I was on a corridor that passed through all of these things.

The road signs caught my special attention. You see, today, I didn't know where I was going. I had called a place for directions, so they told me what to look for and where to exit. There was some construction going on that day, so there were many detour signs, the big orange and black kind with arrows. Fortunately, my path didn't take me on a detour, but a funny thought suddenly struck me — how does anyone know where they will really go by following the signs? What if someone thought it would be funny and repositioned them, and I wound up someplace unfamiliar? What if I wound up where I didn't want to go? For that matter, not only the detour signs but permanent road signs as well. We simply trust the signs to get us where we're going — they are all we have. Wouldn't it be funny to take an exit that said one thing but really ended up somewhere else?

Now, I contemplated life as a road and me driving the corridor. Many things pass quickly, becoming part of the past in a flash before I can give it much thought at all. I wondered how many other people noticed the sunflower's passionate stretch towards the sun. The sight is there, but who besides me saw it? There probably weren't many people who were behind me on the road that day who saw the same thing. Maybe they were looking in the wrong direction to see it; maybe it just blended in with the scenery, and they didn't notice; maybe it was my sign and not theirs.

Life is not a road with directions, but there are signs. Who do we call for directions? How will we know what signs to follow? Nobody has ever traveled down our road before, so who can make the map? The answer is bigger than all of us, and it requires a call to the Master Designer: God. He is the only one who knows where we should be headed and can provide us the compass to our destination. If you call, He will answer. If it's been a long time since you've talked, you might not recognize His voice at *first*, but you will recognize who it is because He doesn't change. As a matter of fact, He just might say something to you that He has said before.

He's waiting, and He has your plans.

www.ingramcontent.com/pod-product-compliance
Lightning Source LLC
Chambersburg PA
CBHW072010290426
44109CB00018B/2196